101 Powerful Tips

For Improving your Credit Score

Pascale Hansen

CONTENTS

Introduction

An excellent credit score is your key to lower rates and easy approval for credit cards and loans. If your credit score has taken a hit, there are some simple strategies you can implement to improve your credit score quickly, starting today.

How long does it take to improve your credit score? It varies and will depend on how bad your credit score is initially. Using the right approach, you can start seeing significant improvements in your credit score in as little as 30 days.

This book will give you a 101 ways to improve your credit score.

There are many misconceptions about credit scores. Some people believe that they don't have a credit score, and many believe that their credit scores are unimportant. These misconceptions can hurt your chances at getting certain types of employment, getting good interest rates, and even becoming a tenant.

The truth is, if you have a bank account and bills, then you have a credit score, and your credit score matters more than you might think. Your credit score may be called many things, including a credit risk rating, a FICO score, a credit rating, a FICO rating, or a credit risk score. All these terms refer to the same thing: the three-digit number that lets lenders and landlords get an idea of how likely you are to pay your bills.

Every time you apply for credit, a loan, a mortgage, certain jobs or a rental property, your credit score is checked. Your credit score can be checked by anyone with a legitimate business needing to do so. Based on your past financial responsibilities, past payments and credit, your credit score provides a quick snapshot of your current financial state.

In other words, your credit score lets lenders know quickly how much of a credit risk you are. Based on this credit score, lenders decide whether to trust you financially and give you better rates when you apply for a loan. Apartment managers can use your credit score to decide whether you can be trusted to pay your rent on time. Employers can use your credit score to decide whether you can be trusted in a high-responsibility job.

The problem with credit scores is that there is a lot of misinformation, some of which is propagated through shady companies who claim they can help you with your credit report and credit score for a cost. From advertisements and suspect claims, people sometimes come away with the idea that in order to boost their credit score, they have to pay money to a company or leave credit repair in the hands of so-called "experts." Nothing could be further from the truth. It is possible to pay down debts and boost your credit on your own, with no expensive help.

The following 101 tips can get you well on your way to boosting your credit score and saving you money.

By the end of this book, you will be able to:

- Define a credit score, a credit report, and other key financial terms

- Develop a personalized credit repair plan that addresses your unique financial situation
- Find the resources and people who can help you repair your credit score
- Repair your credit effectively using the same techniques used by credit repair experts

This book will teach you the powerful strategies you need to build the financial habits that will help you keep a high credit risk rating.

Start reading and be prepared to start taking small but powerful steps that can have a dramatic impact on your financial life.

What Is A Good Credit Score?

A credit score is a 3-digit number that credit bureaus provide to lenders and others who want to assess your creditworthiness. These include banks, mortgage lenders, insurance companies, utility providers, and in some cases, potential employers.

Your credit score can range from bad to excellent. In Canada, credit scores range from 300 to 900, with the following rankings:

- 800 – 900: Excellent
- 720 – 799: Very Good
- 650 – 719: Good
- 600 – 649: Fair
- 300 – 599: Poor

In the United States, the range is from 300 to 850.

If your credit score is ranked in the "good" to "excellent" range, it makes it easy for you to get loan and credit approvals, and qualify for competitive rates.

When your credit score falls in the "poor" to "fair" category, you may be required to pay sub-par rates on credit lines or be denied outright.

What Letters and Numbers Mean in A Rating on a Credit Report

L enders use codes to send information to the credit bureaus about how and when you make payments.

These codes have two parts:

1) a letter shows the type of credit you're using

2) a number shows when you make payments

You may see different codes on your credit report depending on how you make your payments for each account.

What letters mean in a rating on a credit report

Letter	Meaning	Example
I	**Installment Credit** is money borrowed for a specific time period and paid off in fixed amounts until the loan is paid off.	Car loan
O	Open Status Credit Money is available to be borrowed when needed up to a predetermined limit	Line of credit
R	Revolving or Recurring Credit	Credit card
M	**Mortgage** a loan borrowed to purchase real estate	Residential or Commercial Mortgage

What numbers mean in a rating on a credit report

Number	Meaning
0	<ul><li>Too new to rate</li><li>Approved, but not yet used</li></ul>
1	<ul><li>Paid within 30 days of billing</li><li>Paid as agreed</li></ul>
2	Late payment: 31 to 59 days late
3	Late payment: 60 to 89 days late
4	Late payment: 90 to 119 days late
5	Late payment: more than 120 days late, but not yet rated "9"
6	This code isn't used
7	<ul><li>Making regular payments using one of the following debt management options:<ul><li>a consolidation order</li><li>orderly payments of debts</li></ul></li></ul>

	• consumer proposal • debt management program with a credit counselling agency
8	Repossession
9	Written off as "bad debt" Sent to collection agency Bankruptcy

If you have a credit card account that you paid on time, it'll be reported as "R1"

If you have a line of credit, and you missed a payment by 45 days, it'll be reported as "O2"

If you have credit card debt and you're being contacted by a collection agency for payment, it'll be reported as "R9". The best rating is 1. *Any number higher than 1 will likely hurt your credit score.*

The Basics

Before you start boosting your credit score, you need to know the basics. You need to know what a credit score is, how it is developed, and why it is important to you in your everyday life.

Knowing the basic credit score information in this book can help you understand how your everyday financial decisions impact the financial picture lenders get of you through your credit score.

Here are the fundamentals that you need to know:

#1: Understand where credit scores come from.

In general, your credit score is a number that lets lenders know how much of a credit risk you are. The credit score is a number, usually between 300 and 850, that lets lenders know how well you are paying off your debts and how much of a credit risk you are.

The higher your credit score, the better credit risk you make and the more likely you are to be given credit at great rates. Scores in the low 600s and below will often not allow you to obtain credit, while scores of 720 and above will generally give you the best interest rates. However, credit scores are a lot like GPAs as they are interpreted by people in different ways. Some lenders put more emphasis on credit scores than others.

Some lenders will work with you if you have credit scores in the 600s, while others offer their best rates only to those with very high scores. Some lenders will look at your entire credit report while others will accept or reject your loan application based solely on your credit score.

The credit score is based on your credit report, which contains a history of your past debts and repayments. Credit bureaus use computers and mathematical calculations to arrive at a credit score from the information contained in your credit report.

Each credit bureau uses different methods to do this (which is why you will have different scores with different companies) but most credit bureaus use the FICO system. FICO is an acronym for the credit score calculating software offered by Fair Isaac Corporation company. This is by far the most used software since the Fair Isaac Corporation developed the credit score model used by many in the financial industry and is still considered one of the leaders in the field. In fact, credit

scores are sometimes called FICO scores or FICO ratings, although it is important to understand that your score may be tabulated using different software.

The mathematics used by the software is based on research and comparative mathematics. This is an important and simple concept that can help you understand how to boost your credit score. In simple terms, what this means is that your credit score is calculated much like your life insurance premiums.

Your life insurance company likely asks you questions about your health, your lifestyle choices (such as whether you are a smoker or not) because this information allows them to calculate how much of a risk you are (i.e. when you are statistically most likely to pass away) and that will determine how much your premium will cost. The higher the risk the more expensive the premium. Studies have shown, for example, that smokers tend to be more prone to serious illnesses and so require more medical attention. If you are a smoker, your premium will automatically double, compared to that of a non-smoker of the same age and gender.

Similarly, credit bureaus and lenders often look at general patterns. Since people with too many debts tend to have poor rates of repayment, your credit score may suffer if you have too many debts. Understanding this can help you in two ways:

1) It will let you see that your credit score is not a personal reflection of how "good" or "bad" you are with money. Rather, it is a reflection of how well lenders and companies think you will repay your bills based on information gathered from studying other people.

2) It will let you see that if you want to improve your credit score, you need to work on becoming the sort of debtor that studies have shown tends to

repay their bills. You do not have necessarily have to start earning more money. You just need to be a reliable payer.

Credit reports are put together by credit bureaus, which use information from client companies. It works like this: credit bureaus have clients (such as credit card companies and utility companies) who provide them with your payment information.

Once a file is opened on you (i.e. once you open a bank account or have bills to pay) information about you is stored in that file. If you are late paying a bill, the clients call the credit bureaus to notify them. Any unpaid bills, overdue bills or other problems with credit, count as "dings" on your credit report and affect your score.

Information such as what type of debt you have, how much debt you have, how regularly you pay your bills on time, and your credit accounts are all information that is used to calculate your credit score.

Your age, sex, and income do not count towards your credit score. The actual formula used by credit bureaus to calculate credit scores is a well-kept secret, but it is known that recent account activity, debts, length of credit, unpaid accounts, and types of credit are among the things that count the most in tabulating credit scores from a credit report.

#2: Keep the contact information for credit bureaus handy.

The three major credit bureaus are important to contact if you are going to be repairing your credit score. The major three credit agencies can help you by sending you your credit report. If you find an error on your credit report, these are also the companies you must contact in order to correct the problem. You can easily contact these organizations by mail, telephone, or online:

Equifax Credit Information Services, Inc. - www.equifax.com

TransUnion - www.tuc.com

Experian - www.experian.com

You may want to note this information wherever most of your financial information is kept so that you can easily contact the bureaus whenever you need to.

#3: Develop an action plan for dealing with your credit score.

Once you have your credit report and your credit score, you will be able to tell where you stand and where many of your problems lie. If you have a poor score, determine what could be causing the problem:

- Do you have too much debt?
- Too many unpaid bills?
- Have you recently faced a major financial upset such as a bankruptcy?
- Have you simply not had credit long enough to establish good credit?
- Have you defaulted on a loan, failed to pay taxes, or recently been reported to a collection agency?
- Do you have a consumer proposal in place?

The problems that contribute to your credit problems should dictate how you decide to boost your credit score. As you read through this book, highlight or jot down those tips that apply to you and from them develop a checklist of things you can do that would help your credit situation improve.

When you seek professional credit counseling or credit help, counselors will generally work with you to help you develop a personalized strategy that expressly addresses your credit problems and financial history. Now, with this book, you can develop a similar strategy on your own.

When developing your action plan, know where most of your credit score is coming from:

1) **Your credit history** accounts for more than a third of your credit score in some cases. Whether or not you have been a good credit risk in the past is considered the best indicator of how you will handle debt in the future. For this reason, late payment, loan defaults, unpaid taxes, bankruptcies, and other unmet debt

responsibilities will count against you the most. You can't change your financial past, but you can start to pay your bills on time to help boost your credit score in the future.

2) **Your current debts** account for approximately a third of your credit score in some cases. If you have lots of current debt, it may indicate that you are stretching yourself financially thin and so considered much more likely to have trouble paying back debts in the future. If you have a lot of money owing right now and especially if you have borrowed a great deal recently, this fact will bring down your credit score. You can boost your credit score by paying down your debts as much as possible.

3) **How long you have had credit** accounts for up to 15% of your credit score in some cases. If you have not had credit accounts for very long, you may not have enough of a history to let lenders know whether you make a good credit risk. Not having had credit for a long time can affect your credit

score. You can counter this by keeping your accounts open rather than closing them off as you pay them off.

4) **The types of credit you have** accounts for about 10% of your credit score, in most cases. Lenders like to see a mix of financial responsibilities that you handle well. Having bills that you pay as well as one or two types of loans can improve your credit score. Having at least one credit card that you manage well can also help your credit score.

As you can see, it is possible to only estimate how much a specific area of your credit report affects your credit score. Nevertheless, keeping these four areas in mind and making sure that each is addressed in your personalized plan will go a long way in making sure that your personalized credit repair plan is comprehensive enough to boost your credit effectively.

The Best Ways to Boost Your Credit Score

B ecause of the way credit scores are calculated, some actions you take will affect your credit score better than others. Paying your bills on time and meeting your financial responsibilities will boost your score the most. Owing a reasonable amount of money and being able to repay it will show lenders that you take your finances seriously and pose little threat of lost money.

The next four tips (tips 4 to 7) will boost your credit score the most:

4: Pay your bills on time.

One of the best ways to improve your credit score is simply to pay your bills on time. This is absurdly simple, but it works because nothing shows lenders that you take debts seriously as much as a history of paying promptly. Every lender wants to be paid in full and on time.

If you pay all your bills on time then the odds are good that you will make the payments on a new debt on time too, which is what every lender wants to see. Experts think that up to 35% of your credit score is based on your paying of bills on time, so this simple step is one of the easiest ways to boost your credit score.

Paying your bills on time also ensures that you don't get charged late fees and other financial penalties that make paying your bills off harder. Paying your bills in a timely manner makes it easier to keep making payments on time.

Of course, if you have had problems making your payments on time in the past, this will be reflected in your current credit score. It will take a number of months of repaying your bills on time to improve your credit score, but the effort will be worth it when your credit risk rating improves.

#5: Avoid excessive credit.

If you have many lines of credit or several large debts, you make a worse credit risk because you are close to "overextending your credit." This simply means that you may be taking on more credit than you can comfortably pay off. Even if you are making payments regularly now on existing bills, lenders know that you will have a harder time paying off your bills if your debt load grows too much.

The higher your debts, the greater your monthly debt payments and so the higher the risk that you will eventually be unable to repay your debts. Statistical studies have shown that those with high debt loads have the hardest time financially when faced with a crisis such as a divorce, unemployment, or sudden illness.

In order to have a great credit score, avoid taking out excessive credit. You should stick to one or two credit cards and one or two other major debts (car loan or mortgage) in order to have the best credit rating. Do not apply for every new credit line or credit card "just in case". Borrow only when you need it and make sure to make debt payments on time.

Opening lots of new credit accounts in a relatively short period of time will cause your credit score to nosedive because this behaviour will be interpreted as being financially irresponsible.

#6: Pay Down Your Debts

If you have a lot of debt, your credit score will suffer. Paying down your debts to a minimum will help elevate your credit score. For example, if you have a $1,000 limit on your credit card and you regularly carry a balance of $900, you will be a less attractive credit risk to lenders than someone who has the same credit card but carries a smaller balance of $100 or so. If you are serious about improving your credit score, then start with the largest debt you have and start paying it down so that you are using a smaller percentage of your total credit.

In general, try to make sure that you use no more than 30% of your credit. That means that if your credit card has a limit of $5,000, make sure that you pay it down to at least $1,500 and work at not exceeding that balance. If possible, reduce the debt even more. If you can pay off your credit card in full each month, that is the best way to use credit to your advantage and maximize your credit score. What counts here is what percentage of your total credit limit you are using and the lower the better.

#7: Have a range of credit types.

The types of credit you have are a factor in calculating your credit score. Lenders like to see that you are able to handle a range of credit types well. Having some form of personal credit (such as credit cards) and some larger types of credit (such as a mortgage or auto loan) and paying them off regularly is better than having only one type of credit.

Keep Your Credit Score Safe

If you have a lower credit score than you would like, odds are that the score is caused by some small financial mistake, an oversight you have made in the past or being in a circumstance where using the credit was the only option available to you. Not every person with bad credit has a low credit score caused by something they did unknowingly. Sometimes, other people's criminal activity can affect your credit score.

Here are a few tips that can keep you and your credit safe from financial predators:

#8: Look out for identity theft.

Many people who are careful about paying bills on time and having minimal debt are shocked each year to find that they have low credit scores. In many cases, this happens as a result of identity theft. Identity theft is a type of crime in which people take your personal information and steal that information to pose as you in order to get access to your accounts or identity.

For example, someone with your PIN numbers can remove small amounts of money from your bank account each month or someone can use your name and personal information to get credit cards in your name and use those credit cards up to the full credit limit, leaving you with large debt and a poor credit score.

To prevent identity theft, always check your account statements carefully each month. Report any suspicious activity or any charges you don't recognize at once. Also check your credit report regularly and immediately investigate any new credit accounts you do not recognize. This is the best way of detecting identity theft. There are several services that will monitor your credit activity for you and/or allow you to run a report without affecting your score. Borrowell is one such service (borrowell.com) in Canada and Experian (experian.com) in the USA as well as Credit Karma (creditkarma.com and creditkarma.ca).

If you have been the victim of identity theft, report it to the police at once and get a police statement. Send copies of this to your bank and credit bureaus and get the credit bureaus to attach the report to your credit report, if you can. Close all your accounts and reopen new ones. You should not have to pay for someone else's illegal activity.

#9: Practice safe banking, safe computing, and safe business practices.

To protect yourself from identity theft, always follow safe banking and financial practices:

1) Keep account numbers and PIN numbers safe. Cover your account and PIN numbers when using debit at stores and refuse to give your PIN number to anyone. Avoid writing down your PIN and account numbers as you never know when this information could fall into the wrong hands.

2) Only do business with businesses you trust and that you have researched for any potential lawsuits, illegal activity or poor customer service.

3) If you get applications for credit cards in the mail that are "pre-approved" shred the applications and enclosed letters before discarding them. Identity thieves sometimes go through garbage in order to find these forms so that they can fill them out and steal your identity.

4) If you use a computer, install good firewall and antivirus protection systems and update them regularly. Educate yourself about safe computing and best practices for shopping online.

5) Never buy anything online from a company you do not trust or from a company that does not have encryption technology and a good privacy policy.

6) Avoid providing private information through email. Be especially cautious if you get an email from your bank asking you to verify your information by clicking on a link - this is a popular scam that does not come from your bank but from criminals posing as your bank. Ignore the email and phone your bank about the message.

7) Be wary of unsolicited emails, phone calls, or mailed advertisements. Most are from legitimate companies but there are companies who promise you a credit card over the telephone only to charge your existing credit card without sending you anything.

Similarly, letters will sometimes promise you specific items or services. Once you send in your credit card information (usually to a post office box) you hear no more from the company. If you need or want to buy something from a company, be sure to check the company's standing with the Better Business Bureau first.

Send a money order instead of a cheque (which has your account number). If you do use a credit card, report any unusual charges or any payments you made for a product that did not arrive to the credit card company. In some cases, they can stop payment or refund your money as well as take steps to keep your credit card number safe.

8) Be wary of offers that seem too good to be true. If you get an offer for a ten million dollar cheque for which you need to put down money as "a sign of good faith" be aware that this is most likely a scam. Similarly, if you get an offer for a free state-of-the art computer only if you provide your account information, your alarm bells should go off.

Offers that are too good to be true almost always are. Scam artists often rely on your belief in others and your desire to make easy money. They depend on the fact that you will be so excited about a product or service that you will throw good judgment out the window. Prove them wrong. Never take someone up on an offer without doing your due diligence. Investigate the company and the offer.

9) Read the fine print. Some services or companies will have tiny print in their contract or agreement that allows them to charge you extra hidden fees or that allows them to retract certain offers. If you

get an offer through email or the mail, make it a habit to read the fine print.

10) Be alert for a sudden disruption in your mail service. If you do not get mail for some time, contact your post office and ask whether your address was recently submitted for a "change of address" service. One way that criminals steal identities is to change your address at the local post office. They redirect your mail to a post office box number and steal your mail looking for personal information such as bank statements, pre-approved credit card applications, and other pieces of mail they can use to steal your identity.

#10: Check your credit score regularly

You are more likely to notice problems and inconsistencies if you check your credit score on a regular basis - at least once a year and preferably three times a year. Be sure to check your credit rating with each credit bureau. If you notice anything odd or anything you don't recognize (such as a charge account, you did not open) report it immediately.

Sometimes, these errors are caused by mistakes made by the credit bureau, but they could be an indication that someone is using your identity. In either case, such mistakes could hurt your credit score. Fixing such errors improves your credit score.

If you think you have been the victim of identity theft, take action at once:

1) Contact the three major credit bureaus (TransUnion, Equifax & Experian) and ask to speak to the fraud department. Explain that you have been the victim of identity theft (or believe you may have been) and ask that an "alert" be placed on your file. This will let anyone looking at your report know that you may have been the victim of fraud. It will also mean that you will be alerted any time a lender asks to look at your file. Each time a lender does look at your file, it may be an indication that the identity thieves are trying to open a new account in your name.

When the lender sees that the person applying is not you, they will deny the thieves credit and in most cases the criminals will stop trying to access your identity. Most alerts on your file last 90 or 180 days but you can extend this period to several years by asking the credit agencies for an extension of the "fraud alert" in writing.

Sometimes (depending on your geographical location), you can even ask for a freeze to be placed on your credit score and credit report which will prevent anyone but you and the creditors you already have from accessing your file. Any lenders the thieves contact to set up a new account will be refused access and the thieves will not be able to get any more money in your name.

You are entitled to a free copy of your credit report if you have been the victim of identity theft. Be sure to take advantage of this offer so that you can check exactly how your credit has been affected. Dispute those items that are not yours.

1) In the US call the Federal Trade Commission (FTC) at 1-877-438-4338. This is the special

hotline that the FTC has set up to help customers deal with fraud and identity theft. You will be able to get up-to-date information about your rights and advice as to what you can do to improve your credit score and keep in safe in the future. In Canada, report the identity theft to the Canadian Anti-Fraud Centre (CAFC). They provide advice and assistance to victims. Call 1-888-495-8501 or visit antifraudcentre-centreantifraude.ca.

2) Contact the police. Identity theft is a crime and you need to file a police report (be sure to keep a copy of this report) so that you can help the police potentially catch the criminals responsible. Contacting the police will also give you a paper trail and proof that a crime has been committed. Keeping a paper trail of the crime and your response will make it easier for you to repair your credit if it has been damaged by identity thieves.

3) Contact your creditors or any creditors with whom the identity thieves have opened an

account. Ask to speak to the security department and explain your predicament. You may need to have your accounts closed or at minimum your passwords changed to protect yourself.

You may also need to fill out a fraud affidavit to state that a crime has been committed. Keep a copy of this form for your records. The security team of the creditors will be able to advise you as to what you can do. Be sure to note down who you contacted and when so that you have records of the steps you have taken to deal with the crime.

If you have been the victim of identity theft and you are deeply in debt to creditors you never contacted, you will not be held responsible for the charges, but you will have to prove that you have been the victim of identity theft, which is tricky since the thieves are using your name and claiming to be you. It is a frustrating experience because lenders will want to be paid and you will want to avoid paying for charges you did not incur.

Being persistent and keeping good proof that you have been the victim of a crime will help to clear your credit score. In the meantime, however, you will be faced with a much lower credit rating than you deserve, and you may have to put off larger purchases that may require a loan.

Avoid Common Credit Score Mistakes

Follow these tips to avoid the common traps that can sink your credit risk rating:

#11: Beware of debts and credit you don't use.

It is very easy to apply for a store credit card that you forget about in three years. However, that account will remain on your credit report and affect your credit score as long as it is open.

Having credit lines and credit cards you don't need makes you seem like a worse credit risk because you run the risk of "overextending" your credit.

Having lots of accounts you don't use increases the odds that you will forget about an old account and stop making payments on it, resulting in a lowered credit score. Keep only your used accounts and make sure that all other accounts are closed. Having fewer accounts will make it easier for you to keep track of your debts and will increase the chances of having a good credit score.

However, realize that when you close an account, the record of the closed account remains on your credit report and can affect your credit score for a while. In fact, closing unused credit accounts may actually cause your credit score to drop in the short term, as you will have higher credit balances spread out over a smaller overall credit account base.

For example, if your unused accounts amounted to $2,000 and you owe $1,000 on accounts that you have now (let's say on two credit cards that total $2,000) you have gone from using one fourth of your credit ($1,000 owed on a possible $4,000 you could have borrowed) to using one half of your credit (you owe $1000 from a possible $2,000). This will cause your credit risk rating to drop. In the long term, though, not having extra temptation to charge and not having credit you don't need can work for you.

#12: Be careful with inquiries on your credit report.

Every time that someone looks at your credit report, the inquiry is noted. If you have lots of inquiries on your report, it may appear that you are shopping for several loans at once or that you have been rejected by lenders. Both make you a poor credit risk and may affect your credit score. This means that you should be careful about who looks at your credit report. If you are shopping for a loan, shop around within a short period of time, since inquiries made within a few days of each other will generally be lumped together and counted as one inquiry.

You can also cut down on the number of inquiries on your account by approaching lenders you have already researched and may be interested in having as a lender. By researching first and approaching second, you will likely have only a few lenders accessing your credit report at the same time, which can help save your credit score.

#13: Be careful of online loan rate comparisons.

Online loan rate quotes are easy to get. All you have to do is type in some personal information and you can get a quote on your car loan, personal loan, student loan, or mortgage in seconds. This is free and convenient, leading many people to compare several companies at once in order to make sure that they get the best deal possible. The problem is that since online quotes are a fairly recent phenomenon, credit bureaus count each such quote estimate as an "inquiry." This means that if you compare too many companies online by asking for quotes, your credit score will fall due to "too many inquiries."

This does not mean that you shouldn't seek online quotes for loans. What this information does mean, however, is that you should research companies and narrow down possible lenders to just a few before making inquiries. This will help ensure that the number of inquires on your credit report is small and your credit rating will stay in good shape.

#14: Don't make the mistake of thinking that you only have one credit report.

Most people speak of having "a credit score" when in fact most people have at least three or more scores and these scores can vary widely. There are three major credit bureaus in the country that develop credit reports and calculate credit scores. There are also a number of smaller credit bureau companies.

In addition, some larger lenders calculate their own credit risk scores based on information in your credit report. When repairing your credit score, then, you should not focus on one number. You need to contact the three major credit bureaus and work on repairing the three credit scores separately.

#15: Don't make the mistake of closing lots of credit accounts just to improve your score.

This seems like a contradiction, but it really is not. Many people think that to improve their credit score, they just have to pay off some debts and close their accounts. This is not exactly accurate. There are several reasons to think carefully before closing your accounts.

First, if you close an account you need (for example, if you close all your credit card accounts) then you will have to reapply for credit, and all those inquiries from lenders will cause your credit score to drop.

Secondly, most credit bureaus give high favorable points to those who have a good long-term credit history. That means that closing the credit card account you have had since college may actually hurt you in the long run. If you have credit accounts that you don't use or if you have too many credit lines, then by all means pay off some and close them. Doing so may help your credit score, but only if you don't close long-term accounts you need. Close the most recent accounts first and only when you are sure you will not need that credit in the near future.

Closing your accounts is a bad idea if:

1) You will be applying for a loan soon. The closing of your accounts will make your credit score drop

in the short term and will not allow you to qualify for good loan rates.

2) Closing your accounts will make your overall debt balance too high. If you owe $10,000 now and closing some accounts would leave you with only $1,000 of possible credit, you are close to maxing out your credit which gives you a bad credit rating.

In the short term, closing accounts will lower your credit score, but in the long run it can be beneficial.

#16: Don't assume that one thing will boost your credit score a specific number of points.

Some debtors are led to believe that paying off a credit card bill will boost their credit score by 50 points while closing an unused credit account will result in 20 more points. Credit scores are not this clear-cut.

How much any one action will affect your credit score is impossible to gauge. It will depend on several factors, including your current credit score and the credit bureau calculating your credit score.

Usually the higher your credit score, the more small factors (such as one unpaid bill) can affect you. However, when repairing your credit score, you should not be equating specific credit repair tasks with numbers. The idea is to do as many things as you can to get your credit score as close to 800 as you are able. Even if you can improve your credit score by 100 points or so, you will qualify for better interest rates.

#17: Don't think that having no loans or debts will improve your credit score.

Some people believe that owing no money, having no credit cards, and in fact avoiding the whole world of credit will help improve their credit score. The opposite is true. Lenders want to see that you can handle credit, and the only way they can tell is if you have credit that you handle responsibly. If you currently have no credit accounts at all, opening a low balance credit card can boost your credit score providing you can use that card responsibly.

#18: Never do anything illegal to help boost your credit score.

It seems very obvious, but there are many people who lie about their credit scores or even falsify their loan applications because they are ashamed of a bad score. Not only is this illegal, but it is also completely ineffective. Your credit score is easy to check and not only will you not fool lenders by lying, but you may actually find yourself facing legal action as a result of your dishonesty.

Dealing With Your Credit Report to Fix Your Credit Score

If you want to improve your credit score, you need to go right to the source - your credit report. Your credit report contains the information and data on which your credit score is based. If you can alter or update the information in your credit report, your credit score will change to reflect the alterations. For this reason, getting and checking your credit report is one of the first things you should do when you attempt to improve your credit score.

Here are a few tips that can help you deal with your credit report so that you can give your credit score a boost:

#19: Dispute errors on your credit report

Contact each of the three major credit bureaus - TransUnion, Equifax, and Experian - and get copies of your credit reports and credit scores. Carefully read over the reports and note any errors. In writing, contact the credit bureaus and ask that mistakes be removed or investigated. This is called a "dispute letter" and once it is received, credit bureaus have to investigate your dispute within thirty days of receiving your letter. It is important to keep a copy of your letter and note the date the letter was sent. You should not be accusatory or abusive in your letter. Calmly and clearly state the problem and request an investigation.

Note that you are aware the agency is required to investigate the claim within thirty days and note that you will follow up. Be sure that you do follow up with the issues you raised in your letter. An agency investigation does not always mean that your credit report will end up error-free.

Many credit bureaus now make it possible for you to correct errors on your credit report online and many have information on their websites that tells you exactly how disputes must be handled to be effectively removed. It is important that you follow this information exactly so that the inaccuracies on your credit report are removed promptly and your credit score is updated as soon as possible.

#20: Add a note to your credit report if there is a problem you can't resolve

Sometimes there are legitimate reasons why you did not pay a bill. If a contractor refused to finish a job or did a poor job, then you may have refused payment, but the non-payment may still count against you on your credit report. If there are any unusual circumstances surrounding your credit report that may affect your credit rating (such as a case of identity theft) you can ask that a note be attached to your credit report to explain the problem.

Some lenders will pay attention to this and some will not. Such a note will not affect your credit score but will affect your credit report. More importantly, it leaves a paper trail of the problem that lenders can look at if they choose.

#21: Make sure you know who is looking at your credit report and why

Many inquiries look bad on your credit report, but more than that you likely want to know who can see your personal financial information, now that you know that your personal information is stored in a credit report. If you sign a document with a lender or apply for credit online, you can be sure that someone is looking at your credit report. This applies to landlords and potential employers as well. Be aware that when you provide someone with your social insurance number, you may be giving permission to look at your credit report.

#22: Know the difference between soft and hard inquiries

When you pull your credit report to look at it, it is counted as a "soft inquiry." Only "hard inquiries" from lenders will affect your credit score dramatically. So do not avoid checking your credit report because you fear it will make your credit rating worse. It will not.

#23: Contact creditors as well as credit bureaus when correcting inaccuracies in your credit report

When debtors find mistakes on their credit report, they often only contact the credit bureaus. While this is the most effective way to resolve the issue, you should in some cases contact the creditors whose account has caused a ding on your credit report. This can help future dings and resolve problems faster.

Consider an example: Let's say that you were late sending a credit card payment two months ago because you were sick. The late payment is listed as a ding on your credit report even though you have paid it. You should contact the credit bureau in order to get the error removed. However, if you notice that the same credit card company has you listed as having late payments for three months when you paid on time, then it is time to contact the credit card company and ask how to resolve the problem.

The information reported about you to credit bureaus should be accurate and if it is not, then the company extending you credit should work to make sure that they correct the problem so that it does not happen again. You have an advantage in this as the company extending you credit, unlike the credit bureau, depends on your business for their money. They will be motivated to correct the problem or risk losing you as a client.

If you find that a company consistently reports inaccurate information about you to credit bureaus, consider making a formal complaint to the company about it or switch companies. There is no reason why one company's poor organization should cost you your good credit score.

#24: Be aware of where you get your credit report - and what it contains

You can get your credit score from multiple places, one being from credit bureaus themselves. You can pay for the service, but you qualify for one free credit report a year or qualify for a free credit report if you have recently been turned down for credit or if you think you may have been the victim of identity theft.

If you can, get a copy of your free credit report from each of the three major credit bureaus. If you can't get a free credit report, you should still try to get one, even if costs a few dollars. The savings you will enjoy on your loan rates when you improve your credit score will more than pay for the cost of the reports.

There are a number of online companies that offer free online credit reports. These offers are very attractive because you get an online report without having to wait for a report to be sent to you, and you often can get several reports from the different credit bureaus at once, which can save you time.

However, these online companies vary widely, so you will want to compare a few different firms before choosing one. You will also need to read the online company's agreement very carefully as some promise free credit reports only with the purchase of a credit repair program or applying for a loan. In some cases, you can decline the offer and still get the report but in other cases you cannot.

Buyer beware.

Also, some companies will offer you free credit reports that are really a combination of reports from the three major credit bureaus. This is not useful, since you will want to compare each of the three credit bureau reports and fix each credit score separately. You will want to look out for online companies that offer credit reports that are very condensed and you will want to avoid companies that will spam you (send you unsolicited emails) trying to get you to subscribe to some service. Always read the terms carefully to see whether the free credit report offer is legitimate.

If you don't qualify for a free credit report from the credit bureaus, a legitimate online company may be your best option of getting your credit information so that you can start repairing your credit risk rating.

No matter where you get your credit score and credit report, make sure that you get the most complete information package you can. Credit reports are not very exciting or even easy to read. If you are ordering your report online, look for one that includes graphs or lots of details that are easy to understand.

Make sure that you get both your credit report and your credit score. If you just get your report, you will not be able to follow the secret and complicated math formulas used to arrive at your score and the report itself will not make as much financial sense to you if you don't have your score in front of you, as well.

When you do get your credit report you will notice that it contains lots of information about you, including:

1) **Your personal and contact information.** This will include your name and your address, as well as your past several addresses, your social insurance number, your employers (past and present) and your birth date.

2) **Your personal credit information.** A credit report notes all the details of your loans, including the types of loans you have now and have recently had, the dates these loans were opened, the credit limit on each loan, how well you have been repaying those loans (this is important - skipped or late payments count heavily against you in your credit score), and who your lenders are.

3) **Information about you that is of public record.** This may include bankruptcies, unpaid taxes, unpaid child support, tax liens, your dealings with collection agencies, foreclosures, loan defaults, civil lawsuits that you have been involved in, and other information. Much of this will stay on your credit report and will seriously affect your credit score.

4) **Information about who has looked at your credit report and credit score.** Every time that someone looks at your credit score it is called an "inquiry." Your credit report lists who has looked at your credit report in the past two years and how often you have applied for loans and credit in that period of time.

When you get your credit report, it is important that you look at all parts of your credit report and understand what you are reading. Mistakes in any area of your credit report can affect your score, so be sure to check the entire report for inaccuracies and errors.

Dealing With a Credit Score after a Big Problem

Big, bad problems can happen to you - bankruptcies, consumer proposals, divorces, lawsuits and non-payment of taxes. These are big problems that can severely affect your credit score. If you have faced a large problem that has ruined your credit, you need to take action fast and work consistently to boost your credit score.

#25: If you have bad credit, establish better credit by taking out credit and repaying it quickly

If you have terrible credit following a bankruptcy or other major financial upheaval, you may need to get back into a good credit rating by taking out a loan you can handle. Make an appointment to see your bank or bad credit lender a few months or years after the problem in question and arrange for a small loan.

You should have enough savings to pay for the loan before you do this. Pay back the loan quickly. It will not hugely boost your credit score but it will show lenders that you are having an easier time paying your bills. Taking out a small loan you can repay is part of the slow process of reestablishing good credit following a big financial problem.

#26: Try secured credit if you cannot qualify for other types of credit

Secured credit is credit or a loan which uses something as collateral. In some cases, this could be an asset like a house. In some cases, this collateral could be money frozen in an account by the bank for just such a purpose.

If you need credit following a big problem with your credit score, secured credit may be something you can qualify for. You can use this secured credit to reestablish a good credit rating so that you will qualify for other loans in the future. You will have to pay higher interest if your credit score is quite low, but in the long term repaying this type of loan can improve your credit score.

#27: Give it time

Many people believe that simply paying off debts will improve their credit score at once. This is unfortunately not true. If you have experienced a bankruptcy, have been reported to a collection agency, or have had charge-offs, the record will remain on your credit report even after you have repaid your debts.

Major setbacks such as a bankruptcy will remain on your credit report for seven to ten years, affecting your credit score. Even if your credit problems stem from simply not paying bills on time, it will take some time for the mark to fade from your credit report and for your credit score to reflect your better repayment behaviour.

Paying off your debts and resolving problems will help your credit score (since overdue accounts will be marked as "paid" on your credit report), but only time will remove the mark of the problems from your record entirely.

This means that if you have faced a bankruptcy, you will have to wait in order to get the best interest rates on larger purchases. The good news is that the further away you are from a major financial problem, the less dire it appears.

For example, if you have declared bankruptcy, you can expect it to have a huge impact on your credit score for the first two years, during which time you will have a hard time getting any credit at all. However, after two or three years, if you have been paying your bills on time, then the bankruptcy from two years ago will matter less because you have been rebuilding your credit. Your credit will still suffer, but you will slowly be starting to work your way out of the credit problem. Persistence and good financial habits will get you there.

This means that if you plan on making a major purchase (such as a house of car) that may require a loan, you should start working on improving your credit well in advance,- even years in advance of your actual purchase. This is because you simply will not have enough time to radically alter your credit score.

Even if your credit score is already fairly good, you may need to give yourself several months to boost your credit rating enough to get the best loan rates.

#28: Contact your banks and ask credit limits to be reduced.

If your credit risk rating is poor, and especially if it has taken a beating lately due to non-payments or other problems, you can ask that your bank reduce the credit limits on your credit cards, credit lines, and other debts.

You should do this if:

1) **You can pay off at least 50% of your debt loads as they are readjusted**. For example, if you have a credit limit of $5,000 on your credit card and get it reduced to $2,500, you should make sure that you can leave a balance of $1,250 or less. If you owe $4,000 and have no way of repaying it,

getting your credit limit reduced can hurt you. On the other hand, if you need to get a larger loan and can pay off your credit card in full and reduce your limit to $2,500, you may be able to improve your credit score in this way.

2) **You have lots of credit.** If you have several types of debts and credit accounts - lines of credit, credit cards, store charge cards, a mortgage, a car loan, and a personal line of credit, you may be close to overextending your credit, especially if each of these accounts is fairly large. You can't always close down your accounts (especially if you are still paying your debts off) but reducing the limit may make you eligible for a loan should you need it.

3) **You have some credit, but you don't want to close your accounts entirely because you have not had credit for very long.** Sometimes, if you have several types of credit, it is not wise to close them, even if you can, since lenders like to see long-term relationships with lenders. Reducing

the limits can make monthly payments more affordable and can give you a bigger credit boost than closing long-standing credit accounts.

4) **You will not be taking out a loan very soon.** In the short term, reducing your credit limits may actually lower your credit rating because your balances will make up a larger portion of a smaller credit, but in the long run smaller charge accounts will actually boost your credit score by making repayment of loans easier.

#29: Start repairing your credit right away after a big financial upset.

A big financial problem is an emotional as well as a monetary burden. Plenty of debtors feel so terrible about their financial problems and so uncertain about their money that they go into deep denial, refusing to think or work on their financial problems. This will only make the problem worse.

Everybody suffers from financial difficulties at some point in their lives and every professional in the field of finance (from loan managers to bankers) knows this. Financial professionals (including lenders) want your business and so are willing to work with you to help you solve your problems.

If you have had a financial problem, or are even headed towards one, start working on repairing the situation right away. If your credit is suffering because you have not paid some bills, for example, don't make it worse by waiting until you are reported to a collection agency (by which time your credit rating will have taken an even worse hit). Instead, work on paying off your bills or arranging a payment schedule right away.

#30: Consider co-signing for loans - but consider well before taking the leap.

If you have a very poor credit score following a bankruptcy or consumer proposal, but need to get a loan, consider getting a co-signer. If your co-signer has assets or a better credit record, you may not only qualify for a loan but get a better rate.

However, be wary. Co-signers share responsibility for loans and credit. If your co-signer refuses to make payments, then both of you will suffer the credit fallout. Both of you will have worse credit scores if one of you does not pay. The risk of getting a co-signor is not just financial. If you renege on your payments and your co-signor has to pay your debt, then your relationship is at risk as well. Think carefully before you ask anyone and make sure than you honour your commitments.

#31: Don't overlook bankruptcy.

A bankruptcy is a legal proceeding that either forgives you of your debts or allows you to pay off just a small fraction of your debt. It will ruin your credit rating initially but may be the only way to survive from crushing debt and allow you to start fresh and work towards re-establishing good credit. It will take up to ten years before a bankruptcy no longer shows up on your credit report. In the meantime, you may not be able to get any loans, credit cards or jobs that require good credit.

If you are very seriously in debt and have no way of repaying your bills, a bankruptcy can help you by stopping collection agencies from calling you. Also, if you have been very negligent in paying your large debts, your credit rating has already likely suffered greatly. While a bankruptcy will depress it even further, at least it will give you the chance to repair your credit by giving you a "clean slate" free from large debts.

#32: Don't choose bankruptcy as an easy out. Consider a Consumer Proposal.

Bankruptcy is a serious credit problem. It is not just a "ding" on your credit report, it is a huge red flag to lenders. After a bankruptcy, you will be ineligible for credit cards, many types of credit and will even be told what you can and cannot buy. The procedure of bankruptcy can also be emotionally draining. Bankruptcy should only be chosen as a last option if you really require your debts to be forgiven because you have no way of repaying them.

An alternative to bankruptcy that is less severe is completing a consumer proposal which is a formal, legally binding process that is administered by a Licensed Insolvency Trustee (LIT). In this process, the LIT will work with you to develop a "proposal" which is an offer to pay creditors a percentage of what is owed to them, or extend the time you have to pay off the debts, or both. A consumer proposal can reduce your debt by as much as 80% and if it is paid off early may only stay on your credit report for 3 years (depending on the laws in your state or province).

#33: Learn from your mistakes.

Everyone makes mistakes and it is very rare for someone to go through their entire lives without at least a few dings on their credit risk record. Don't beat yourself up over your mistakes, even if they are large ones. Instead, learn from your mistakes by analyzing them and asking yourself how you can improve. Think of your credit mistakes as clues which can help you in the future by avoiding the same behaviour.

- Do you develop credit problems because you overspend while shopping?
- Are you so disorganized that you forget to pay bills?
- Are your bills simply too large for your current income?
- -Do you routinely get overcharged for things and fail to notice until much later?

Knowing what your mistakes are and finding solutions to the problems can go a long way towards helping you develop a good credit risk rating.

Professional Credit Help

Credit repair is big business, and there are many companies that will promise to help you get out of bad credit problems. There are a number of legitimate resources that can help you in improving your credit score but there are also a number of less than reputable companies that will take your money but offer you few (if any) valuable services.

A few basic tips will help you see the difference:

#34: Seeking professional help

If you are in over your head, and your credit is so bad that you cannot get a loan and may even be facing bankruptcy, you may want to seek help from professionals. There are a number of financial professionals that can help you with credit repair including:

Certified Cash Flow Specialists can help you with day-to-day money management to maximize your cash flow in the short and long term and help with debt repayment plans.

Money Coaches help you clarify your goals and design a detailed, integrated financial plan that details debt repayment, minimizes your taxes and increases your wealth in order to achieve those goals.

Credit repair companies and credit counseling companies: These companies can help you by acting on your behalf with credit companies and helping you with consumer proposals.

Bankruptcy lawyers and bankruptcy advisors: Bankruptcy lawyers can help represent you in bankruptcy proceedings. Advisors can help you decide whether to apply for a bankruptcy and how to proceed once you do decide to file.

Bad credit lenders: will give you credit usually with some collateral in place and will help you establish a better payment history. This will (in time) help you get better rates with regular lenders such as banks.

#35: Look out for credit repair companies.

Many companies advertise that they can help you with credit repair, but the quality of these services varies widely. Some companies really can help you with credit repair while others may be under investigation for suspect business practices. If you decide to seek help from a credit repair company, be sure that the company is legitimate and offers you viable services.

Check that the company has a good standing with the Better Business Bureau and positive reviews from clients who are satisfied with the credit repair services they received. Always read the paperwork carefully before you sign and make sure that you understand what you are paying for and how much you are paying.

Before deciding to seek help from a credit help or credit counseling service, be sure that the problem cannot be resolved on your own.

Indications that you may need credit counseling include:

- You cannot pay your bills and avoid the necessities of life.
- You avoid the phone, the mail, and the door because you are being harassed by collection agencies.
- You have avoided going out because you feel terrible about your financial state.
- You have no idea how you will repay your bills and loans and you do not know where to start.

#36: Seek free or inexpensive help before seeking paid credit repair help

If you need credit repair, the odds are good that your finances aren't in the best possible shape and you are better off spending as little as possible on fixing your credit. The money you save can be channeled into repaying your debts. Before seeking credit repair services, follow the tips in this book in order to repair your own credit.

Also, seek out free or inexpensive sources of credit repair help. Some non-profit credit counseling services are registered charities and will work on your behalf. If you can get help from one of these companies or undertake credit repair yourself, you will be able to save money. In addition, these companies tend to be more legitimate than credit repair companies that charge a fee.

37: It will be easier for financial experts to help you if you seek credit repair help sooner rather than later

If you do decide to seek credit repair help from the experts, it makes sense to seek that help before your financial situation spirals too far out of control. After all, credit repair experts can do little for you if your credit and financial situation is so bad that the only option left to you is bankruptcy.

#38: Look out for credit repair scams

Credit repair scams are widespread, so always do your research. These scams often promise to help free you of bad credit, when in reality the "experts" offering these services will either overcharge you, involve you in illegal activity, or actually put you in a worse financial situation.

Look out for these most common scams:

1) Credit repair companies that tell you to lie on loan applications or suggest that you develop a second identity. This is illegal and dishonest. If a company suggests that you open accounts in a new name or falsify your information on loan applications, run away. You can be charged with fraud for doing this and you will be held responsible for your actions, even if you were acting under the company's advisement.

2) Credit repair companies that charge you fees or hidden fees for things you could do for free yourself such as get a credit report.

3) Credit repair companies that promise to pay your creditors from money you pay to them and which they keep in an escrow account. This is a common scam and it presents a huge problem for the debtor.

Here's how it works: the debtor gives money to the credit repair company, presumably for paying off debts.

The company places the money in an escrow account where it earns interest. The idea is that the company will eventually pay off your debts when the amount reached in the account matches the debts. The problem is that in the meantime, the credit repair company is withdrawing money from the account for administrative fees while creditors are becoming more and more anxious, increasing the interest on the debts and even starting legal action against the debtor. This type of "credit help" can actually ruin your credit rating.

1) Credit repair companies that pressure you, don't listen to you, or want you to sign a contract you have not read. Such companies are not to be trusted.

2) Companies that offer you fast or instant credit repair, no matter how bad your credit. This is simply a false claim that no company can legitimately deliver on. If you have very bad credit, it may take years to fully repair.

In many cases, these companies will claim that they can remove your poor credit history from your credit report by disputing it. This is highly inaccurate. You simply cannot remove correct information from your credit report. It is true that a credit bureau must investigate a claim of erroneous information within thirty days, but this does not mean that the company will automatically remove the information.

In fact, if the information is accurate, the data will stand. Credit bureaus are aware of this common credit repair scheme and have become very good at detecting it. Many credit repair companies (and even some individuals) will try to dispute every ding on a credit report, hoping that the backlog of disputes will cause the credit bureau to automatically remove the offending items from the report (the credit bureau is legally required to remove disputed items it has not investigated within 30 days). This technique is dishonest and will not work. Refuse to do business with credit help companies that use this practice.

#38: Get a good team on your side to help you with your credit score

A good team of professionals can help you get your credit score back in shape. The most important member of your team is you. No one will care more about your financial well-being than you. Using the information in this book you are well-equipped to become your own best advocate in credit repair. You may also want to include financial experts such as credit counselors or a money coach to help you.

If you decide to seek a team of experts to help, be sure that you check each person's credentials and standing with their professional associations. Anyone you work with should be a financial fiduciary which means that they have the responsibility of acting in your best interest, putting your needs ahead of their own with a duty to preserve good faith and trust. Beyond this, make sure that you sign a contract or agreement with each professional member of your team.

#39: Your bank has good and reliable credit information

One free and professional source of credit information is your bank. Your bank manager may be able to offer you professional, free advice, especially as banks are trying harder and harder to provide good personal service to their clients.

Your bank may also have a number of credit solutions (such as overdraft protection) that can help you maintain good credit. Banks and credit unions are realizing more and more of their clients are dealing with less-than-ideal credit and are trying to meet the demands of this new group. This means that they can be a powerful ally for those who are trying to improve their credit.

General Good Financial Habits Build Good Credit Scores

Developing good financial habits can help your credit score by putting you in a good financial position.

These financial habits are especially credit-friendly:

#40: Creating a Spending Plan

One of the biggest reasons that people develop poor credit is overspending. In many cases this overspending is caused by not working with a spending plan, not tracking where money goes and where and how expenses can be minimized. A spending plan will keep this in check and include tracking debt repayment and savings goals.

Getting and staying debt-free with a strong credit score takes planning, commitment and discipline. All plans should be realistic and allow for pleasurable activities within income streams.

#41: Living within your means

Many people believe that if they only had more money, they would not have to worry about credit. This is just not true. Many people who have money (or at least have all the trappings of money, including expensive cars and luxurious homes) have terrible credit. This is because it is not your income that decides whether you are a good credit risk or a bad one, but rather how you handle money. You could be earning $14 per hour and still paying your bills and meeting your financial responsibilities, in which case you will have terrific credit. You could also be earning $300,000 a year and be in terrible debt due to unpaid bills and excessive debt.

The best way to ensure that you have a good credit rating, regardless of your income, is to spend less than you earn. That means living below your means. If you have a very small income, you may need to live with roommates in order to keep costs down. If you have a medium-sized income, that may mean saving more and entertaining less.

Your income is not a factor in determining your credit score. Although your past and current employers are listed on your credit report and lenders may be able to guess your income from your loan amounts, the simple truth is that your income does not count.

This means that if you won the lottery today or suddenly inherited a large sum of money, your credit score would not increase. With your credit rating, what matters is how you manage your money, not how much you make.

#42: Get out of the spending habit

We are surrounded with advertisements that tell us to buy, buy, buy. Stopping spending consciously can be hard, just like with any new habit, but it's possible and necessary to achieve financial independence.

If your desire to be financially organized is strong enough, it only takes a decision to get started and progress to keep going. Often partnering with someone with the same goal to help keep you accountable is very helpful. Saving your money by spending less can let you pay off your debts faster, which will improve your credit score.

#43: Save

One of the best ways to ensure that your credit rating stays good is to save money each month. Whether you are able to save $25 a month or $200 or even more, the habit is more important than the amount as long as there's a realistic minimum. The amount can always increase.

Once you have an opportunity fund, (a fund that gives you the opportunity to stay debt-free by having 6-12 months earnings for living expenses in case you lose your job or have any unexpected expenses), you can start investing what is left over to grow your wealth and prepare for retirement or financial independence.

#44: Keep track of your money

Most people are surprised by how quickly their money seems to be spent. This is because impulse spending and small-purchase spending adds up quickly. Small-purchase spending is small spending we do without even thinking about it such as buying a coffee or a magazine we don't need.

Impulse spending refers to simply buying things we don't use or need. In both cases, we end up spending too much unnecessarily, and this is a problem in credit repair because you want to be channeling as much money as you can into savings and debt repayment so that you can improve your credit.

For a month, try keeping a daily record of every penny you spend. Include the money you spend on tips, online, everything. You will be amazed at where your money goes.

Keeping track of your money this way does two things:

1) It automatically cuts down on spending. If you have to write down where you spend your money, you will be much more careful what you spend your money on.

2) It allows you to see where your money goes and take steps to stop the bad habit. If you notice that you always buy the newspaper on Saturday but

never read it, for example, you can stop buying the paper on that day. Small savings can add up over the years and can put you in good financial shape which will be reflected in your credit risk rating.

#45: Reduce pleasure spending and saving instead

- Do you have cable?
- Do you subscribe to lots of magazines?
- Are you still paying for gym memberships you don't use?

We all entertain ourselves with money, but most of us have at least one or two things that we have either outgrown or don't enjoy as much as we once did. Cutting that expense and saving that money is a good habit that will pay off. If you give up your cable television, for example, you can pay off your credit cards that much faster, improving your credit score.

#46: Build assets and capital

Whether it is buying a car, a home, or creating an investment portfolio, having assets can help improve your credit score by allowing you take out secured credit, or credit in which your assets are used as collateral.

When you take out secured credit (such as a mortgage) you enjoy lower interest rates and easier approval. As you repay your secured debt, your credit score will improve. Lenders look at the types of credit you have. If you have a mix of secured and unsecured credit, you will enjoy better risk rating scores as it will indicate that you have the means to repay your debts.

Building assets and capital is also a way of building financial stability which can help protect your credit score. If you have assets such as savings or investments, then you have a way of generating income or repaying debts in case of an emergency. You also have ready money you can use in case of unexpected medical bills or other expenses.

#47: Find more ways to earn income

While you are repairing your credit, you will want to channel as much money as you can into savings and debt repayment. For this, having a second income or even just a few hundred dollars a month more can mean that you get your credit into shape faster.

Having a secondary form of income can also keep your credit safe. If you lose your job, you can use the money you make from a secondary source to repay your bills until you find another form of employment.

There are many ways to get more income:

- You can ask your employer for a raise.
- You can start to sell something online.
- You can establish your own small business part-time.
- You can get a part-time or weekend job.

Whatever you do, finding an alternate source of income can help your credit immensely.

#48: Prepare for financial emergencies

Few of us think about what would happen if we lost our jobs or suddenly became too ill to work. The thought is simply too terrible to contemplate in many cases, especially if we are living paycheck to paycheck in our current job.

Unfortunately, financial emergencies happen to almost everyone at some point and they can have a devastating impact on your credit. In fact, most people who declare bankruptcy do so because of a huge financial disaster such as sudden unemployment, huge medical bills, a lawsuit, or divorce. Despite this, few people plan for these problems even though there are ways to manage these risks.

#49: Get overdraft protection, insurance on your credit cards, or other services to keep your credit in good shape

Talk to your bank and lenders about services they offer to keep you safe. Overdraft protection, for example, is a basic service that often costs nothing or very little. It will protect you in case you withdraw too much money from your bank account.

When you have overdraft protection, you do not get a "ding" on your credit report or a charge for insufficient funds. In most cases, you get a day or two to add more money to the account to cover the gap. Some credit cards and other loans offer a similar service or offer insurance which protects you in case you lose your job and are unable to pay your bills for a few months.

#50: Get insurance

Insurance for health, your car, your home, and for liability can help you avoid the huge legal and medical bills that can occur from an accident or critical illness. For a monthly fee, you can be covered against unexpected events that can drain your finances and leave you with out-of-control debt.

#51: Get a prenuptial agreement and a lawyer to review your business contracts

Most bankruptcies are caused by the fallout that occurs as a result of business failures, lawsuits, health costs, and divorces. Getting a prenuptial agreement helps to ensure that a divorce will not adversely affect your finances and lead to a ruined credit rating.

Keeping accounts separate while married is also a good idea, as your spouse's own financial troubles can all too easily become your own. Having a lawyer look over contracts can at least reduce the risks of unfavorable agreements that can put you at a disadvantage in business or marriage.

Think Like a Lender

If you think like a lender, you can see which habits and traits you need to develop in order to be considered a good credit risk. Thinking like a lender will help you understand how you must manage your money to be appealing to them.

Here are a few tips that can put you in the right mindset:

#52: Know how money works

Reading books about money and understanding how your accounts and loans work can go a long way towards helping you keep your credit in good shape. For example, if you know that some loans will charge you extra if you pay off your loan faster while others will not, you will be in a better position to make financial decisions.

The more you know about money in general, the more comfortable you will feel with it and the better decisions you will be able to make. This will help improve your overall financial situation and will help you keep your credit stellar.

You don't need to do extensive research to appreciate how money works. One easy way to consider money is to think of it the way you think of time. You likely hate to waste time and you want to make the best use of it as possible. Apply the same attitudes to your financial life and watch for the difference it will make.

If overspending has caused you to have a bad credit score, consider thinking of the money you spend in terms of how long it would take for you to earn that amount. For example, if you make twenty dollars an hour, then a magazine subscription of $20 will represent one hour of your work. Imagine an hour of your work and ask yourself whether the subscription is worth the time it took for you to earn it. Do that with everything you spend. How many times is the answer "No" and what could you do with the money you save? Once you start seeing money as something that comes from your hard work, impulse spending will seem much less attractive, and it will be easier to keep your credit card limits low.

#53: Take care of those things besides a credit score that affect how lenders view you

Lenders will often look at not only your credit score but at other financial indicators, such as your income, employment record, and savings. Keeping these things in order can complement your credit score.

Be aware that when a lender asks to see your credit score, the credit bureaus send not only your credit score, but also the top four reasons why your credit score is lowered.

The most common reasons for lowered credit scores are:

1) Serious delinquency in paying accounts or bills.

2) Public record of bankruptcy, civil judgment, or report to a collection agency

3) Recent unpaid or late paid debts or accounts

4) Short-term credit record

5) Lots of new accounts

6) Many accounts have late payments, defaults, or non-payments

7) Large debts or amounts owed.

Knowing that your lender sees these possible problems can help you see the need to develop the best possible face to present to a lender. Lenders who look at your entire credit report may get a more positive picture of you than lenders who see only a number and four reasons for a lower score.

#54: Follow up on closed accounts

You closed a store card years ago, but is it still listed as an open account? Bureaucratic mix-ups happen, often quite frequently. If you want to keep a good credit score, you need to follow up on financial details.

Whenever you close an account, whether it's a credit account, bank account, or utility company account, make sure that you get written confirmation that the account is closed and paid in full. Make a note to yourself to follow up with the company a few months later to confirm the closed account. This simple precaution can save you hours of frustration not to mention a lowered credit score.

#55: Don't move around a lot

Lenders like to see stability in regards to your housing as it suggests stability in financial matters, making you a better credit risk. Every time you move, you may have to change your credit information including switching banks. This negatively affects your credit score by not allowing you to develop long-term relationships with lenders.

Remember that your current and past addresses are listed on your credit report even if they do not directly affect your credit score. Any lender looking at your full credit report will be pleased to see that you create a stable life for yourself. Not moving too frequently can also save you money on moving costs, which can add up quite quickly.

#56: Don't change jobs frequently

Of course, there will be times when you will have to change jobs. However, avoiding changing jobs unnecessarily will help improve your credit score by allowing you to stay in one place and build a steady financial picture.

Your credit report shows your current and past jobs and if a lender sees that you change jobs frequently, s/he may wonder whether you have the life stability required to handle debt responsibilities. Also, the lender cannot see why you left a job. If there are many employers listed on your credit report, the lender may wonder whether you have been fired from jobs and whether that is an indication that you will be unable to pay your debts due to unemployment at some point in the future.

A lender makes their money by the interest charged on a loan. If you default on a loan, you cause the lender to lose money. Above all, the lender wants to see evidence on your credit record that you have the traits that will make you repay the loan.

Frequent job changes may indicate to some lenders that there is a likelihood that you will simply disappear with the money or default on a loan. Having a stable life including a longer-term job and one place of residence typically indicates to lenders that you are building roots and be unlikely to move and default.

#57: Avoid switching credit companies and credit accounts frequently

Credit companies will often offer you special introductory rates, generous gifts or other incentives to switch companies. However, you should resist the temptation unless you have a reasonable reason to switch. Establishing a good credit relationship with one company (having one credit card from your college days, for example) is a good way to show lenders that you are likely to take money matters seriously. That is exactly what lenders want to see. Switching accounts and lenders makes you appear fickle and less than reliable.

#58: Keep your records up-to-date

Not knowing what is going on in your own financial life is courting disaster. Keep one file folder which contains your financial information and review this periodically. If something changes in your life like getting married, starting a family, moving or changing jobs, look through your financial folder and contact everyone who needs to be contacted to update them on the change. This will help ensure that all your creditors have the information they need about you. Keeping your own records up-to-date will help you make sure that everyone who handles your finances is also up-to-date.

#59: Always be sure that your creditors know your current address

If you move and forget to inform all your creditors of your new address, you may not get all your bills, making you look like a delinquent debtor and making your credit score plummet. Make sure that you either close your credit accounts or get your new address and contact information to your creditors.

When you move, make sure that you inform credit card companies, stores you have credit cards with, banks and anyone else with whom you conduct financial business. Better yet, also arrange with the post office to have your mail automatically forwarded to you at your new address. This will ensure that any creditors you may have overlooked will still be able to contact you, and you will have a second chance to remind them of your address change.

#60: Talk to lenders and creditors

Many people are hesitant to keep an open line of communication with their lenders because they are embarrassed about their financial state or because they feel unsure about what to say.

Lenders do not know that you cannot make a payment. They simply see that you have failed to make a payment which may indicate a temporary problem or a decision on your part to default on your loan.

Without your input, your creditors have no way of knowing what the issue may be and since their profits and money are at risk, they tend to assume the worst. Keeping the lines of communication open as soon as a problem develops can help reassure your lenders and can help your creditors see that you are responsible with the money they are owed.

Talking to lenders as soon as a problem develops can be an effective way to prevent a ding on your credit report that can affect your credit score. For example, if you are having trouble paying your bills, you can often work out a more reasonable payment schedule.

In most cases, you will not get a ding on your credit record if you do this because the lender will have some assurance that your financial obligations will still be met. In fact, one of the things that most credit repair companies do is to arrange for more reasonable payment schedules. A simple phone call is all it takes.

Lenders want, above all, to be repaid so that their interest rates can earn them a profit. By communicating whenever there is a problem and showing that you are willing to work hard to meet your responsibilities, you show your creditors that they will get their money and this makes lenders more willing to work with you to ensure that your credit rating is not badly affected by one missed or late payment. Speaking with your creditors can help establish a good working relationship that can help keep your credit rating from dropping.

#61: Ask lenders to waive late fees and charges

If you have missed some payments or made some late payments, lenders will often charge you a fee for non-payment. This not only adds insult to injury - you have to pay more on your bills and get a ding on your credit - but also makes bills more difficult to repay since the bills are now higher. You can phone the lender and ask to have the charge waived. This is a secret that credit repair companies have long known and is one of the first services they will perform on your behalf. You can easily do this yourself, at no cost.

Lenders want to get paid, and if they think that you will pay your bill more quickly by waiving the late fee, they will often gladly remove the fee in exchange for prompt payment.

Develop an Organized Strategy to Repair Your Credit Score

Staying organized is very important when you are trying to boost your credit score. A few basic organizational tips can help make sure that you do not overlook anything that can put your credit score at risk:

62: Stay financially organized

Keep all your financial records (including tax records) in one place. Note the days you paid your bills on the bills themselves. Note how much you owe and where you owe money. Keeping your financial information in one place allows you to refer to it easily. Seeing all aspects of your financial life in one place also makes it easier for you to see where your credit and your financial life still needs work.

The information you want to keep in your financial file include:

- Bills
- Tax receipts and returns
- Your credit reports and scores
- A list of financial contacts (your banker, accountant, tax preparer)
- Your written financial plan
- Banking information
- Financial forms
- Investment information
- Deeds to houses
- Agreements you have signed for loans and other financial services
- Insurance policies
- Power of attorney

You may want to keep your separate information in different labeled folders (tax information together, for example, and bills in another folder) for easy referencing. Whatever system you use, you will find it much easier to manage your finances and your credit if you don't have to hunt for random pieces of paper when needed.

#63: Set short-term goals and do frequent credit self-checks in order to track your progress

Credit repair takes time and effort. Some days, it will seem that you are getting no closer to a better credit score at all, but in time you'll get there. In order to manage your progress and keep moving, you need to set goals and keep track of what you are doing.

For example, setting a goal such as "I will improve my credit score" is far too broad. Set smaller goals, such as "I will talk to my banker about budgeting this week" or "I will pay off half my credit card bill by next month." These goals work better because they are specific and have a deadline.

Writing your goals on a calendar or planner you look at everyday will motivate you to keep working on your credit repair and taking the small steps needed to reach your goal. If you review how far you have come each month or week, you can easily keep track of your progress.

#64: Be meticulous with the details when requesting your credit report

Little things make a big difference. Misquoting your social insurance number or using a slightly different name (Jane Doe Smith instead of Jane Smith) can make a big difference, since credit bureaus can count the two names as different people. Making sure that you fill out each financial form accurately and in the same way, can go a long way in ensuring that there are no mistakes in identity that can affect your credit score.

#65: Don't make the mistake of thinking that small differences in credit scores or loan interest rates won't make a big impact

A few points on a credit score can mean the difference between a lender offering you a prime rate reserved for the best credit risks and the worse interest rate offered to less- than-prime customers. This may amount to only a few percentages in different loan rates, but this can have a huge impact, especially on a large purchase. For example, a few percentage points on a long-term fixed-rate loan can mean the difference between tens of thousands of dollars saved or tens of thousands of dollars overspent.

It is in your best interest to boost your credit score by every percentage point you can and to fight for the lowest interest rate loans you can get. If you have larger payments each month due to a higher interest rate than you deserve, it will be harder for you to repay your bills. Also, you will qualify for fewer loans if you have higher-than-needed interest rates, as you will not be able to afford the larger monthly payments.

#66: Stay organized with a to-do list that ensures you don't forget anything

As you can likely tell by now, credit repair is not one magical solution but rather lots of relatively small things you can do to help repair your credit. To make sure that you don't overlook anything, you may want to develop a to do list that you can post and check off.

You may list credit accounts you need to close, accounts you need to pay down, people you need to contact, and things you need to check out or research. As you tick off each item, you will get a sense of accomplishment knowing that you are taking steps to improve your finances. Keeping a credit repair checklist posted will also keep you on track and let you know what you still need to do.

#67: Automate your finances

Thanks to automatic bank payments, you can have your bills taken out of your checking account every month. If you get dings on your credit report because you can never remember to pay your bills on time, this can be a very useful service.

You can even set up your email service to send you automatic reminders of bills that are due soon so that you can pay them on time. This sort of automation makes it easier to keep your credit score clean if your credit score suffers mainly from your own forgetfulness or disorganization.

Loans and Your Credit Score

Loans affect your credit score more than almost any other item on your credit report. The types of loans you have, how long you have had the loans, the amounts you owe and your payment history on your loans has one of the biggest impacts on your credit score. If you can control your loans, you can boost your credit score.

Here are a few tips that can get you well on your way to painlessly managing your loans:

#68: Refinance loans

If you got a poor deal on a loan (especially a major loan such as a car or mortgage) or if your credit rating has improved since you got your loan, you may want to consider refinancing. Refinancing means that you take your loan to another lender in order to enjoy better terms or rates.

You don't want to do this too often as it prevents you from developing long-term relationships with lenders and results in inquiries on your credit report. However, if you have good reasons to refinance, it can help you repay your debts faster. For example, if you can get more reasonable monthly bills that you will be able to repay, refinancing can help prevent all those non-payment credit dings that come from not being able to pay your bills. Making your payments more affordable can save you money and can save your credit score.

In the short term, refinancing can push your credit score down, as you will acquire inquiries on your credit report as you look for a new lender and as you close old accounts and open new accounts. In the long term, though, refinancing can be a good way of boosting your credit score.

#69: Look for loans that are offered for bad credit risks

If your credit score is bad but you need a loan, consider services that cater to people with poor credit scores. These companies know that some creditors with poor credit scores will still make their payments on time and so are willing to speak with debtors other companies would reject. You will be charged higher interest rates but choosing a bad credit lender can go a long way to ensuring that your credit score won't disqualify you for a loan. In the long run, you can always refinance your loan to take advantage of a better rate once your credit score improves.

#70: Always know your credit score before speaking to lenders

Many people assume that having an excellent credit score is enough when applying for a loan. It is not. Some lenders are not interested in offering you the best rate, especially if they can gain by having you pay higher interest. They may tell you that your credit score is lower than it is and that this disqualifies you from a better rate. Some may rely on your ignorance (or what they think is your ignorance) about your credit score to quote you a higher rate.

Never let a lender do this. Always look up your credit score before shopping for a major loan and if you are quoted a rate you think is unfair, speak up and tell the credit officer that your credit score of 700 (or whatever the score is) seems to indicate a better loan.

Show the lender your printed copy of your credit score. If the lender tries to tell you that lenders get more accurate credit scores than customers who look up their own credit scores or that your credit score has changed, walk away. There are many reputable lenders. Find one of them rather than relying on a lender who is just trying to make a bigger profit.

#71: Consider speaking to lenders face-to-face if you have a bad credit score

If you apply for a loan over the phone or online, your credit score will count the most, because that is all the lender will likely look at before getting back to you with a quote. If you have bad credit but still need a loan, meet with a lender face-to-face if possible. This is better because an actual meeting allows a lender to get an impression of you and allows you to explain the problems you have had in the past. If you make a good impression, it will likely be harder to decline you to your face. On paper you will be just another number whereas in person, the lender will be interacting with you as an individual and be affected by your personality, your story and your communication style.

Make Credit Repair Easier on Yourself

Credit repair is no picnic. It requires continual work and effort to get a good credit score and to improve a bad one. You will stand a much better chance of getting a better credit score if you make it as easy on yourself as possible. In many cases, people actually have low credit scores not because of carelessness or indifference, but because hectic lifestyles lead to oversights and missed credit payments. There are several things you can do to make good credit almost automatic:

#72: Don't let a bad credit score make you avoid purchases you have to make

You will make life much harder on yourself if you deny yourself things you need (such as medical treatments) because your credit is poor. If you have bad credit, but need money for something urgent, consider a secured loan or a bad credit loan with fair terms. Do not let bad credit affect your ability to stay safe and healthy.

Some people think that getting credit while trying to repair their credit score is a bad idea. While it is true that you will not get the best interest rates on loans before your credit score is improved, getting loans that you need may simply be too important to put off.

#73: Make arrangements to pay your bills when you are on vacation or ill

Make it part of your vacation practice to pay bills in advance or to arrange for someone to pay your bills while you are away. Similarly, while you are ill, arrange to have bills paid so that bills don't pile up and you get marked as a "non-payer." It is frustrating to be trying to improve a credit score only to suffer a setback over a small oversight.

#74: Consider online banking to make bill payment easier

If you have trouble getting your payments in on time, consider online banking. This simple system is now available from virtually every bank and can help you pay your bills in minutes at any time of the day or night. If you travel a lot, online banking can be a real life-saver as it will allow you to pay your bills no matter where you are.

Plus, you get instant confirmation of the paid bill and your payment is counted instantly. You no longer have to worry about payments getting lost in the mail or getting lost in a bureaucratic shuffle. The record of the payment is recorded on your bank account statement.

#75: Simplify your bills

You can often get great discounts by choosing to get several services from the same company. For example, a package deal from your phone company can give you internet access, long distance phone plans, and cable television all on one bill at a bundled rate. Pooling your insurance into one package from one insurance provider can have the same effect. Reducing the number of bills you get can make it easier for you to pay your bills and so reduces the chances that your credit rating will be affected by non-paid or late-paid bills.

#76: Pay your bills as soon as you get them

If you leave your bills until later, you may forget and end up being listed as a late payer. Some companies may not report you to credit bureaus right away, but others report even one skipped or late payment, which can show up on your credit report and affect your credit rating. Most companies, including utility companies and credit card companies, offer paperless statements so they will be delivered right to your inbox. This allows you to get your bill right away and cuts down on the amount of mail you get.

#77: Set aside a regular day, time, and place for paying bills

If you are too busy to pay your bills as they arrive, set aside one hour each week for paying your bills and organizing your finances. Have the same place and time set aside each week, so that paying incoming bills and taking care of your finances becomes an automatic, good habit.

#78: Record your financial tasks on a calendar - just like all your other appointments

If you mark down when bills are due, when you need to make payments, and what you need to accomplish to boost your credit score in a visible place you check often, you are less likely to overlook important appointments and deadlines.

#79: Go online for credit information

There are a number of online resources that can help you find credit information and can help you with your credit repair project:

The FICO web site - www.myfico.com - contains lots of useful credit repair information and even allows you to order credit reports and scores.

The credit bureaus (transunion.com, equifax.com and experian.com) allow you to order credit scores and credit reports online as well as giving you information on reporting errors on your credit report.

Student Credit Repair

Students are increasingly worried about credit and credit scores and for good reason. Student debts are rising and the numbers of students who leave school with ruined credit scores is rising as well. Many experts blame larger credit card debts and rising tuition costs that lead to larger student loans.

Despite the pressures of today's students, it is possible to leave school with a good credit score and in fact to develop good financial habits that can lead to a lifetime of good credit ratings.

Here are a few tips that can make the college years a credit-booster instead of a credit disaster:

#80: If you are a student, you have a great secret weapon for credit repair and credit help - your school's financial aid office

If you are a college student, your school's financial aid office should be one of your first stops on campus. Few students visit this office regularly while they are in school and this is a mistake. The financial aid office at most universities and colleges has information to help you keep your credit score in good shape.

Most financial aid offices offer one-on-one financial counseling, information about scholarships, tips on budgeting, books on money, and many other resources including workshops that can teach you about dealing with money and credit. Some even offer free tax-filing services.

The financial aid offices at most colleges and universities are so useful that you may want to call the school you attended to ask whether alumni are eligible for any services that they offer.

#81: If you are a student (and especially a student with student loans), budget carefully

Student loans need to be paid back and are increasingly for large amounts. Taking out the smallest loans you can and sticking to a budget can help establish good credit habits that can help ensure that you have a good credit score when you leave university.

#82: Try to pay for education through means other than loans

As tuition fees rise, larger student loans are becoming the norm which creates a financial burden after graduation. Although most student loans do not have to be repaid until after graduation, the time after graduation usually carries some new financial responsibilities. Many college graduates want or need a car, a job, and possibly accommodation. Each of these things requires a good credit standing, but very large student loans not only require bigger monthly repayments but also may affect credit scores by overextending credit.

To avoid the financial burden that large student loans can become, take out the smallest loan you can, secure part-time jobs, dip into savings, apply for scholarships, bursaries and other forms of financial aid to make up the rest of what is needed for your tuition and living expenses. You should rely on loans as a last (not a first) option.

In general, need-based, government-subsidized student loans generally offer the best terms and rates. After that, college and student loans from private lenders may offer decent rates. Personal loans and credit cards should only be used when absolutely necessary to pay for an education, as these tend to have higher interest rates and require that you start repaying them right away.

#83: Avoid defaulting on a student loan

Some students think that defaulting on a student loan after graduation is a smart way to get rid of a debt. It is not. Defaulting on a student loan is a terrible mistake because it affects your credit rating very negatively and for a long time. If you have student loans, it is important that you start repaying them on schedule and that you repay them on time. Doing so will improve your credit score.

If you are having trouble repaying your student and college loans, speak to the lenders rather than ignoring the problem. Most lenders will give you a six-month grace period after graduation so that you can find a job and settle into post-college life before repaying your loans.

If you have several loans, your lenders may be willing to help you pool them into one larger loan payment that requires smaller monthly payments. Some lenders will also give a few months grace in case of unemployment.

#84: Save money by taking advantage of student discounts

One of the advantages of being a student is being able to save money with student discounts. Student housing or rooms rented with roommates will decrease your accommodation expense. On-campus facilities offer services at discounted rates, and many businesses offer student-only deals.

Try to take advantage of these offers to make your student money stretch further so that you can take out the smallest student loans possible. Look around to find the best student-deal offers from your campus and from surrounding businesses.

#85: Follow the "cash for wants, loans for needs" rule

Many students fall in love with their credit cards. Credit card companies know this and heavily advertise on college campuses, even offering students free food or gifts to fill out a credit application. While the convenience of credit cards is tempting, it is a good habit to use credit cards only for major purchases, saving cash for entertainment, food, clothes, and other everyday expenses. Studies have repeatedly shown that those who pay cash for items, regularly spend less than those charging purchases on their credit cards. Using only cash or debit for entertainment and other small needs ensures you won't spend more than you have.

#86: Make learning about money a priority

Whether you attend information sessions at the financial aid office, read about money in books or take courses, learning how to manage your money is an important part of life and one that will go a long way to not only helping you minimize the stress in your life, but giving you the tools to create the life you want.

For many students, their time away from home is one of the first times they are responsible for finances. Learning to handle this responsibility well as a young adult ensures that you will enjoy a good credit standing your whole life. Learning about money will also help you prevent costly credit mistakes.

#87: Start building credit early and do it well

Start building credit early, before starting college, if you plan on taking out student loans. Ask your parents to sign over a bill that you pay on time each month. Get a credit card with a low limit and a bank account that you balance each month. Avoid opening several charge cards at once. Not only will they be hard to repay, but having several new accounts when you have a short credit history will actually cause your credit rating to drop. Get a part-time job.

Each of these things can help you establish good credit, which in turn can help you get a good student loan rate. More importantly, establishing credit early will help ensure that you have a long (and good) credit history by the time you graduate from university, which will help you with all your important, large post-graduation expenses.

Dealing with Debt

Debt is a major factor in your credit score. If you have too much of it (or none at all) or if you have trouble repaying your debts on time, your credit score will plummet. Keeping your debts reasonable and paid on time will do more than almost anything else to improve your credit score.

Here are a few tips that can ensure that your debts help you boost your credit score:

#88: Consolidate your loans to make repaying them easier

Having lots of loans and debt are the biggest reasons leading to poor credit ratings. The larger your debts, the worse your credit rating and the more likely that you will find yourself with large monthly bills that are difficult to repay.

Consolidating your loans means that you take out one large loan to repay all your creditors so that you only have one large loan to repay. While the overall amount of the loan does not change. If you owed $20,000 to five different companies, you will still owe $20,000 but to only one lender, but the interest rates and monthly payments are usually smaller and this can help meeting your debt obligations much easier.

Debt consolidation can be an especially good idea if you have lots of high-interest debt. One smaller monthly payment will be easier to remember and will help make bill payment time less painful.

#89: Pay down your debts by making larger than minimal payments

If you only pay down the minimum amount on each of your loans, it will take you a long time to pay them off. This is because most lenders only require that you pay down slightly more than the interest amount on your debt each month. Even a debt of a few hundred dollars could take several years to repay this way.

Paying down your debts by putting down more than the minimum required monthly payment can help you pay down your debts faster and so can boost your credit score. Paying down more than required also shows lenders that you are in good financial shape and conscientious about your debts which are two qualities that make you an attractive credit risk to lenders.

#90: If you are taking out a new loan, consider putting down a larger down payment to minimize your loan

Doing all you can to take out a smaller loan by putting down a larger down payment or buying a less expensive car or home (if that is what the loan is for). This can help ensure that you don't overextend your credit and that your monthly payments on the debt will be reasonable and affordable to you.

In fact, for larger purchases, some debtors take out piggyback loans, most often for a mortgage. They borrow money for a down payment, so that they can get a better rate on the larger second loan they take out to pay for the purchase.

Do your math before making a big purchase. You may find that a larger down payment (even if you have to borrow to get it) can help your credit by making your payments more affordable and by ensuring that you don't overextend your credit.

#91: Use loan calculators to determine your payments and interest rate

Online loan calculators are a useful tool that can help you determine how much of an interest rate you should pay, how much in monthly payments you can afford, and how much your loan will cost you in interest over the long term.

There are online loan calculators for auto loans, home loans, and personal loans. If you are going to be getting a new loan, these calculators can be a helpful resource.

#92: Avoid payday loans

Payday loans are also called "cash advance loans" and they are small and short-term loans that carry extremely high interest rates. Some companies have even begun to advertise them as loans to help you repair your credit, but this is very misleading. Payday loans can have the exact opposite effect because if you cannot afford to pay your payday loans on time, you have to "roll-over" or extend the loan with enormous interest. Many people get into a payday loans cycle, whereby much of their monthly paycheck goes towards paying off their ever-growing payday loans, interest and fees, creating a constant stressor that has no end date in sight. Do everything to avoid getting into this trap.

Several states are investigating payday loans for possible illegal activity stemming from usury laws. If you cannot afford your bills one month, you are much better off trying to arrange an alternate schedule of payment with the companies you owe money to rather than risking your credit rating through payday loans. Payday loans cycles quickly become unaffordable and can ruin your credit rating in addition to making your life miserable. Watch the Dirty Money documentary episode called Payday (season 1, episode 2) on Netflix to learn more and hear from people's experience with payday loans.

#93: Do not use one debt to repay another

This results in accumulating interest and possibly to unpayable bills. If you use one credit card to pay off another you are paying interest on interest, and paying off the new credit card bill will be more difficult. This method will also mean that you will always be looking for new credit and new debt to pay off your increasing debts. It makes more sense to get a second job or arrange for a new payment schedule.

Paying off your debts with another debt may help you in the short run in that you will not have a late payment on your credit record, but in the long run the larger debt load will make maintaining good credit more and more difficult. The only exception to this rule is debt consolidation, in which all your bills are paid by one lender, who then becomes the only creditor you owe money to.

Credit Repair and Your Emotions

Unless you learn how to manage your emotions you will never be able to fully manage your life or your money. It may be difficult, but it is possible and definitely worth the effort. You may think that money is all about being rational but in fact our emotions are very often what drives us to success or disaster. If you want to repair your credit, you have to deal with the emotional side of it, not just the numerical side.

Here are a few tips that can help you harness your emotions in a way that can help you improve your credit score:

#94: Give Yourself a Break

There is no point in beating yourself up over your credit score. Instead, promise yourself that you will do better in the future and then work to repair your credit rather than working on berating yourself. Taking action to improve your credit rating will improve your outlook as well as your credit.

#95: Don't make excuses

If you have been the object of identity theft or have genuinely been mistreated by a company, then by all means include an explanatory note in your credit report. Whatever your problems have been in the past, you will seem much more reliable to a lender if you focus on what you are doing to work on your problems.

You will feel better and get more favourable responses from lenders if you focus on current action rather than past mistakes. Instead of wallowing in pity and explaining in great detail the personal and financial problems that led to a bad credit rating, give yourself and lenders the condensed version and then move on to a detailed review of what you are doing to repair your credit.

#96: Give Yourself a Treat - without affecting your credit rating

Re-establishing good credit is hard work. As you reach a milestone, you need to reward yourself with something that does not involve incurring debt. What can you do for yourself that's inexpensive and enjoyable? Make a list of those things and keep it in your financial file. As you reach a big milestone, take out your list and immediately reward yourself with one of the items on the list. This will not only keep you motivated, but it will inexpensively keep you from feeling too deprived while you work on your credit score.

#97: Work on your emotional response to debt and money

Most of us carry a lot of emotional baggage with us when it comes to money. We see money as a marker of success, or we see money as a way of making ourselves feel better, and these attitudes often lead us to our financial and credit problems. If we rely on money to make us feel successful, then we are apt to overspend.

If we fear money, we are unlikely to save it or make investments with it.

We need to be aware of the ways we respond to money and the ways that those responses shape the ways we deal with money. Keeping a money journal documenting what you spent money on and how you felt at the time of the transaction can help you by showing you how you feel about spending and about money in general. If you can isolate the emotions that influence how you spend money and how you make your money decisions, it will be a starting point to help you become aware of underlying money issues. Working with a money coach will also help you address the underlying psychological issues around money management.

#98: Don't mix debt with emotion and stay aware of your emotions

It pays to separate your feelings of worth and your emotions from your finances, especially when you are trying to repair your credit. Feeling self-pity, shame, fear, or sadness as you try to repair your credit score won't help you. Staying calm and professional as you deal with credit bureaus and financial professionals will help you. Remind yourself that although your credit score is an important number, it's not a reflection of who you are as a person and does not define your worth. You can change the number to your benefit. It takes commitment, information, patience and discipline. No number tells you who you are nor can it define your value as an individual. That's always up to you.

Bad credit can be emotionally draining and boosting your credit can be daunting and difficult as well. It is important that you keep track of your emotions during the process. If you find yourself dwelling on your credit too much or if you find yourself severely depressed, seek help at once. A credit problem, like all other problems, has a solution.

#99: Get help if you need it

Do not be afraid to ask for help (financial or emotional) if you need it. There are a number of wonderful organizations that can help you. If you have credit problems due to compulsive overspending, for example, Spenders Anonymous and Debtors Anonymous can be of great help.

If you suffer from a gambling problem, there are a number of charitable organizations that can help you overcome the addiction. If you have accumulated debt as a result of these specific problems, you will not be able to fix your credit rating unless you deal with the problems underlying the bad credit. Many good groups, therapists and money coaches are out there that can help you.

Parting Credit Tips

Before you head off to enjoy your new and improved credit score or to work on boosting your credit score, consider two more tips that may well come in handy as your try to repair your credit score:

#100: Learn to deal with collection agencies

If you have bad credit, you will have to deal with collection agencies sooner or later, and these companies often present the most persistent and unpleasant problem for those with bad credit. Collection agencies are basically companies that work on behalf of companies to try to recoup money that is owed.

If you owe your credit card company a payment that has not been made in some time, your credit card company will eventually ask a collection agency to speak with you. In many cases, collection agencies try to get money for their clients through phone calls.

Some collection agencies are quite reasonable and will try to work with you. However, some will use threatening or harassing techniques including verbal threats and daily phone calls to try to get you to pay.

When dealing with collection agencies, always get the full name of whomever you speak with at the agency. Be honest about your ability to repay and try to work out a payment schedule or payment options. If at any point you feel threatened or harassed, end the call. Hang up the phone if the collection agent persists and make direct contact with the company who is trying to recoup money from you.

Get the name of the collection agency and report them and the agent you spoke with to the Better Business Bureau. Refuse further calls from the collection agency and continue your communication with the creditor directly, noting each time the collection company contacts you with harassing or abusive calls.

Unfortunately, some collection agencies feel that intimidation yields the best results and since most collection agencies work by calling, they feel that they can say whatever they like (including making personal and false accusations) in order to try to recoup money for their clients. There is no paper trail and few people harassed by the agencies take these companies to court.

Some debtors feel so ashamed of their bad credit rating that they almost feel that they deserve the abuse. That view is completely wrong. A bad credit rating does not make you someone who deserves abuse. Report collection agencies that offer harassment as a technique and make it clear to lenders that you will not work with a company that uses abuse as a technique for recouping money.

Some collection agencies will try to use your credit score against you, telling you that they can ruin your credit score or file a claim on your credit score. Don't fall for this. Your credit score is instantly affected when you fail to make a payment or are reported to a collection agency, but there is nothing that the collection agency employee can do to make your credit score worse. Do not let false claims about your credit score intimidate you into accepting the abuse of a collection agency.

#101: Keep at it

Credit repair is not something that you simply do once in a while when your credit rating slips. Credit repair and credit check-ups need to be part of your overall long-term financial plan. You need to follow a regular maintenance schedule of checking your credit reports. You can get one free credit report from each of the major credit bureaus every four months, which lets you check your credit for free three times a year.

Regular check-ups will ensure that you have not been the victim of identity theft and will help you make sure that your credit has not begun to drop. Catching errors and problems early can be an excellent long-term way to ensure that you never need intensive credit repair again.

Your credit should be part of your financial goals because your credit can help you meet your goals. Good credit can help make loans affordable and so can help make acquiring education, homes, and cars possible.

Overall, you should continue to follow the strategies in this book in order to develop good habits that will keep your financial life stable and will help keep your credit score strong.

Conclusion

Developing your own plan for credit repair is the most cost-effective and often the efficient way of dealing with bad credit. By being persistent and following the tips in this book, you can turn your credit situation around and make your financial life much easier.

Start reestablishing your credit today so that you can get on track with living the stress-free life you want and deserve.

Wishing You Massive Success,

Pascale

About The Author

As a money coach and cash flow specialist, Pascale Hansen helps people with their financial lives, starting with education. Her book 101 Powerful Tips for Improving Your Credit Score is written to help people understand how credit reports and credit scores work and what can be done inexpensively to improve both, in order to get better terms and interest rates for loans and credit.

Pascale possesses a BA degree in Psychology from the University of British Columbia in Canada. She has found her calling in the financial services industry and her goal is to promote financial literacy, financial planning and helping people stretch their money further, so that they can live more abundantly.

Pascale Hansen, Money Coach

Money Coaching for Financial Independence

lesstaxmorecash.com

www.ingramcontent.com/pod-product-compliance
Lightning Source LLC
Chambersburg PA
CBHW070551220526
45467CB00003B/1161